Paul Reeve on Race & Priesthood

Introduction

I'm excited to have Dr Paul Reeve back on the show! He's the author of a new Deseret Book called "Lets Talk About Race & Priesthood." We're going to dive deep into the priesthood and temple ban, and we're going to highlight some early black Mormons you probably won't be familiar with. We'll also talk about some exceptions to the ban, including the son of a slave who was ordained in 1971! Paul discusses justifications for the ban, and how he responds to those claims. You won't want to miss this conversation....

Tags: Gospel Tangents, Rick Bennett, LDS Church, Latter-day Saints, LDS Church, Mormon, Mormon Church, Church of Jesus Christ of Latter-day Saints, Mormon history, Mormon, LDS Church, LDS, Church of Latter Day Saints, Paul Reeve, Let's Talk about Race & priesthood, race ban, temple ban, early black Mormons, Deseret Book, temple, Brigham Young, Orson Pratt, John Taylor, Joseph Smith, Elijah Abel, Elijah Able, African ancestry, enslaved, slavery, Wilford Woodruff, black ordination, Enoch Lewis

Contents

Introduction 2

Intro to Isaac Manning 5

Century of Black Mormons 9

Isaac Van Meter 11

Joseph Ball 13

Walker Lewis 16

Enoch Lewis 18

Moroni Able 19

Enoch & Elijah Able III 21

Warner McCary 24

Russell Dewey Ritchie 26

Black Pete 32

One Drop Rule..36

Hardest Book Paul Has Written 38

Wilford Woodruff "One Drop" Problem 42

How Deep Into the Ban? 47

Rapid Fire Questions About Book 50

Orson Pratt Rejects Curse of Cain 52

Death of Elijah Able...54

Jane James' Attempt at Temple Blessings 57

Joseph F Smith Solidifies Restrictions 59

How 1978 Revelation Affected Black Women 60

Addressing Lingering Justifications of Ban..62

Additional Resources: 67

    Dr. Paul Reeve on Black Mormon History in Utah 67

    Critiquing the LDS Gospel Topics Essays 68

    Darron Smith on Race, Religion, & Sport 69

    Russell Stevenson – Biographer of Elijah Abel, early black Mormon missionary 70

    Newell Bringhurst – Author of Saints, Slaves, and Blacks 71

    Matt Harris – Black History WW2 to Present....................................72

    Race Struggles at BYU 1965-1985 73

Final Thoughts..74

Intro to Isaac Manning

Interview

GT 00:36 Welcome to *Gospel Tangents*. I'm excited to have one of my favorite historians. It's been a long time since he's been on the show. Some of you new listeners may not have even known that Paul was my second interview ever.[1] Paul, could you go ahead and tell us who you are and where we are?

Paul 00:52 I'm Paul Reeve and I'm a Simmons Chair of Mormon studies in the history department at the University of Utah.

GT 01:00 Perfect. I remember the last time I talked to you, you had just received a promotion. And this is not the same office that we were in last time.

Paul 01:12 That's right.

GT 01:13 I think you've received a couple of promotions since then. Last time you were a full professor. What's happened in the last seven years?

Paul 01:20 So I am now chair of the History Department at the University of Utah. It's a three-year appointment. I'm in the first of three years as chair at the department.

GT 01:32 And that's your favorite job?

Paul 01:35 Well, I'd probably rather be in the classroom.

GT 01:40 You know, it's funny because Margaret Toscano, she's been on a couple of times, and she was department chair.[2] And she was like, "I can't wait until I'm done with this."

---

[1] See https://gospeltangents.com/2022/09/paul-reeve-discusses-race-ban/

Paul 01:48 Yes.

GT 01:49 What's the big deal about department chair? Why is it such a terrible job?

Paul 01:54 {Chuckles} Well, hopefully no one from my department listens to this. It's a lot of bureaucratic work that just isn't my favorite thing.

GT 02:05 Okay. I can see that. So, you're just much more of a researcher.

Paul 02:10 Yeah, I'd rather be in the classroom and researching and writing.

GT 02:15 Well, very good. Okay. Well, you've got a new book. Now, why don't you go ahead and show it to the audience? It's a big book, you can see.

Paul 02:24 (Chuckling) It's very small.

GT 02:25 What's it called?

Paul 02:26 Let's Talk About Race and Priesthood.[3] It's a part of Deseret Book's, "Let's talk About" series. Darius Gray wrote the foreword and I'm really honored to have his story at the beginning of the book. He's a remarkable Latter-day Saint and I'm really honored that he was willing to participate and write the foreword.

GT 02:57 Yeah, Darius is a great guy. I actually talked to him when I saw you last week at Writ & Vision. So, he's going to be on the show. But for those people who don't know who he is, could you just give a short blurb about Darius?

Paul 03:11 Yeah, Darius joined the Church of Jesus Christ of Latter-day Saints before the 1978 revelation and has been just an important black Latter-day Saint ever since. He was a part of the original Genesis group leadership and became president of Genesis, which is a support group for black Latter-day Saints officially organized by the Church. He was a counselor from 1971 to 1997. So, think about the tenure that he spent there. And then he became president of Genesis from 1997 to 2003.

GT 03:55 You know, they used to have 20-year callings. We didn't think those still were around, but apparently, they are.

Paul 04:00 In Darius' case, they were, yes. And he really became the face of Genesis and really made it what it is today. I think he's lived through being a black Latter-day Saint and all of the changes that the 1978 Revelation brought about and is really remarkable.

GT 04:28 He's a great guy. I'm looking forward to talking to him, so that'll be a lot of fun. The other thing I want to mention, behind you, I'm going to scroll up a little bit. Tell us who is on the painting behind you here.

Paul 04:42 So this is Isaac Lewis Manning, Jane Manning James's brother, who converted to the Church of Jesus Christ of Latter-day Saints in Connecticut, within a few months of Jane's conversion. [He was] part of her family that embraced the gospel and he went to Nauvoo with Jane and the rest of the family. He became a cook for Joseph Smith and Nauvoo Mansion House. And then, at the murder of Joseph and Hyrum, Isaac dug four graves. He dug two graves that were decoy graves where caskets were filled with sand were buried because they were afraid that the mobs that killed Joseph and Hyrum would come back and desecrate the bodies.

Paul 05:35 Then he dug the actual graves where the bodies were buried at the Joseph Smith homestead. And so, Marlena Wilding is the artist who did this portrait of Isaac. She included the shovel as the symbol of Isaac's service. And it's such an important act of service to him, that in 1903, after he had arrived in Salt Lake, he swore out an affidavit that gave the details of his service in digging those graves. And so that affidavit is what is he's holding in his other hand, so [he is holding] the two symbols of his service. He considered it his badge of honor that he provided this service for the slain bodies of Joseph and Hyrum.

GT 06:24 Everybody knows about Jane, but I don't think anybody knows that story about Isaiah, her brother, so that's pretty cool.

Paul 06:29 Yeah, he's got his own remarkable story. I wrote an article on him in the *Journal of Mormon History*.[4] So you can read more about that. And then there's a shorter version at The Century of Black Mormons database.[5]

---

[4] See https://scholarlypublishingcollective.org/uip/jmh/article-abstract/47/1/29/219224/I-Dug-the-Graves-Isaac-Lewis-Manning-Joseph-Smith?redirectedFrom=fulltext
[5] See https://exhibits.lib.utah.edu/s/century-of-black-mormons/page/manning-isaac-lewis

Century of Black Mormons

GT 06:43 Okay. And I was glad you mentioned *Century of Black Mormons*. That was my next question. Tell us a little bit about that.

Paul 06:49 So I am manager and general editor for an online database. It's a website. It's just www.centuryofblackmormons.org. We are just attempting to identify all known people of black African descent, baptized into the Church of Jesus Christ of Latter-day Saints in its first 100 years, between 1830 and 1930. We have 130 biographies completed and publicly available in the database, and 200 more under research. So, by the time we're done, we'll be somewhere between 300 and 400 in the database. We write biographies. We also load all primary source documents that we find and have permission to make publicly available, so that the general public can see the documents, but also read the biographies of these black Latter-day Saints.

GT 07:50 Now, that brings up another question, two questions. First of all, since Isaac is behind you, let's talk about him first. Was he ordained to the priesthood, that you've been able to identify?

Paul 08:02 No, Isaac was not ordained to the priesthood. He stays in the Midwest when Jane migrates to Utah with her husband, Isaac James. Isaac Manning stays in the Midwest. Eventually, in 1876, he moved to Canada, and joins the Reorganized Church of Jesus Christ of Latter-day Saints. They allowed black priesthood ordination, but like the Church of Jesus Christ of Latter-day Saints, they didn't practice universal priesthood ordination in the 19th century. Meaning that, in the 19th century, both churches basically ordained enough men to run a given branch or Ward but didn't practice universal ordination. That's true for the Church of Jesus Christ of Latter-day Saints, that doesn't really change until they start to systematically ordain young men at age 12, around 1908. And then you have the almost universal male ordination that becomes systematic in the 20th century but wasn't the case in the 19th century. So, the fact that there were black priesthood holders in the 19th century, when not all white men were ordained, makes it that much more remarkable. But Isaac was not ordained in the Church of Jesus Christ of Latter-day Saints or the Reorganized Church of Jesus Christ of Latter-day Saints. The Reorganized Church did ordain black men to the priesthood in the 19th century, but only to support a branch structure and they eventually develop segregated congregations in the south, presided over by black priesthood holders but segregated from their white congregations.

GT 09:52 Oh, so, they kind of had a black church and a white church, essentially.

Paul 09:55 They did.

GT 09:56 That's interesting. I didn't know that.

Paul 09:57 Yeah.

Isaac Van Meter

GT 09:59 Another question that I want to ask, this is kind of a personal question. I've been trying to research a guy named Isaac Van Meter. Is he in your database? Does that name ring a bell?

Paul 10:11 That name sounds familiar, but we don't have a biography on him.

GT 10:15 Okay. Here's why he is important to me. I know there was a DVD done by Margaret Young and Darius Gray, "Nobody Knows."[6] And in the extras on that video, the Connell O'Donovan, had mentioned Isaac Van Meter. I think he said [Isaac] was a missionary companion to Wilford Woodruff, I think somebody like that, [Lorenzo] Snow, maybe. And he thought that Isaac Van Meter was an early black Mormon. I haven't been able to get a second opinion on that. So, does that ring any bells?

Paul 10:30 No, it doesn't. But we should certainly add him to our research list. We have a list of people who are potentially people to be included in the database, and then we do the research. And if the evidence bears it out, then we write the biography, and they're included. But I don't think he's even on our research list.

GT 11:22 Oh, really?

Paul 11:23 Yeah.

GT 11:23 So I gave you a tip.

Paul 11:26 You gave us a tip. Yeah. Send us the information. And we'll put him on the research list at least.

---

[6] Can be purchased at https://amzn.to/3FQwVBX

GT 11:32 Because he's one of six--we were just having lunch. Maybe I will take you up on that. I want to write a book on this because it's one of my favorite topics. Including Isaac Van Meter, I've been able to identify six-ish, but I'm not nearly as good of a researcher as you, Paul.

Paul 11:52 You're probably better. I mean, it sounds like it. Yeah.

Joseph Ball

GT 11:55 But the six that I've identified, and I would like you to address them really quickly, Elijah Able,[7] of course, everybody knows about him. Joseph Ball, you've actually found some information on him. Because in our first interview, I had said, "Well, Joseph Ball[8] was the first black high priest in Boston." You pushed back a little bit on that. And I know you've done some research since that interview. Can you share a little bit about Joseph Ball?

Paul 12:24 Sure. We didn't find any evidence that those who associated with Joseph Ball knew him to be black. In other words, there is evidence that he was of black African descent, but that he and his sisters passed as white. And Jeffrey Mahas did the research and the biography for this entry of Black Mormons database,[9] and I think did a really good job. But no contemporary sources that anyone in the Latter-day Saint community understood him to be black, that he had passed as white. So, people like Wilford Woodruff who were associating with him don't ever mention him to be a person he understood to be black. But, in other situations, Woodruff does mention, for example, Q. Walker Lewis[10] as a black elder, and he creates a membership record when he goes through Tennessee and 1835. Actually, in some of the branches, he draws a line and then says "Colored saints" and includes the names of five black Latter-day Saints in 1835, in Tennessee. So, it just feels improbable that he would be a companion with Joseph Ball and never mention in any sort of way that he understood him to be black.

GT 13:56 Because he did mention Walker Lewis, as you said.

---

7 See https://gospeltangents.com/tag/elijah-abel/

8 See https://gospeltangents.com/2017/02/22/the-black-mormon-scandals/

9 See https://exhibits.lib.utah.edu/s/century-of-black-mormons/page/ball-joseph-t

10 See https://gospeltangents.com/2018/02/26/walker-lewis-faithful-black-elder/

Paul 13:58 He does, and he does single out these other black Latter-day Saints who are in the branches in Tennessee and identifies them specifically as colored. In the public records for Joseph Ball, none of them identify him as black after he passes as white into adulthood.

GT 14:23 So, it's likely that he was ordained, assuming he was white.

Paul 14:28 Yeah, yeah. So that's another thing we do in the database. We trace people who, because the church implemented what came to be called a one-drop policy, meaning trying to exclude anyone with what was considered, in the 19th century, one drop of African blood is how they described it. Right? We now have DNA. We don't understand things the same way. But that's how they described it, meaning you could have 99 White ancestors and one black ancestor, and you would still be qualified as black. Some states adopted one drop rules during the segregation period to legally define a person who was black. Well, the LDS Church does so in trying to define and ferret out temple admission and priesthood ordination. So, because they had that policy for inclusion in the database, we include anyone that we can verify of any African ancestry. And so, Joseph Ball is...

GT 15:24 Even if they passed as white in this case.

Paul 15:25 Even if they passed as white. If we can verify African ancestry, and Joseph Ball's case, that's easily done, because his father is of African ancestry.

GT 15:38 He's from Jamaica, I believe.

Paul 15:39 Yeah, he may have been a mixed racial ancestry. So that it makes it easier to understand how, by Joseph's generation, he and his sisters were able to pass as white, because probably the product of a couple of generations of interracial marriages, but nonetheless, African ancestry and therefore qualifies for the database. But we don't have evidence that those who ordained him to the priesthood were aware that they were ordaining a black man to the priesthood, in other words.

GT 16:11 Yeah.

Paul 16:11 So it just illustrates, like several other cases in the database, the impossibility of policing racial boundaries.

GT 16:20 Okay. And I think that's important. I'm really glad you did that research, because Connell, I think, is a great historian. And he was the one I had learned that from. I was always under the impression that he was an open black man and was openly ordained, but it sounds like that really wasn't the case.

Paul 16:39 Yeah, we've had no evidence of that.

Walker Lewis

GT 16:41 But Walker Lewis was a barber, and I think it was Wilford Woodruff, mentioned him. He was openly ordained.

Paul 16:48 Absolutely. Yeah. Yeah, incontrovertible evidence. A letter that that Wilford Woodruff writes, calls him a colored elder. And [he] does so as if there's nothing unusual about this. And then other people who visit that branch--he's hosting missionaries in his home, having potential investigators into his home for missionaries to have meetings with. He's paying a really generous tithe. We found his tithing records. He, at one point, pays a trombone in a trombone box as tithing. He was a musician and had a variety of musical instruments. And at one point, I guess, the trombone became tithing, as well, but he must have done well in his barber shop in Lowell, Massachusetts, because he was paying a generous tithe in the 19th century. And [he's] ordained, most likely by William Smith, who was an apostle at the time, Joseph Smith's younger brother. Other apostles who visit the Lowell, Massachusetts branch, just acknowledge him as a black Elder.

GT 18:13 Do we know approximately when he was ordained?

Paul 18:15 Yeah, it's 1843 or 44?

GT 18:18 Okay, so right before Joseph's death.

Paul 18:20 Yeah, before Joseph's death, but there's no surviving document to know for sure. And so, it really depends on which visit to the Lowell branch that you count. William Smith, he's there in 1843, so he [Walker Lewis] could have been ordained then. He's there in 1844, he could have been ordained then. It's later that William Appleby goes and says that he was ordained by William

Smith. And it's because there's no surviving documentation, it's likely 1843 or 1844.

GT 18:54 Well, it's interesting, because I believe it was 1845 when Joseph Ball was made the branch president. Does that sound right?

Paul 19:02 That sounds about right, yeah.

GT 19:04 Because I've always wondered--there was a lot going on in that branch. That's kind of a soap opera itself.

Enoch Lewis

GT 19:14 Okay, so we've identified, if we can't Isaac Van Meter, Elijah Able, Walker Lewis. His son, Enoch Lewis, was also ordained. Right?

Paul 19:22 His son Moroni.

GT 19:23 Moroni, I thought it was Enoch.

Paul 19:25 Oh, oh, sorry. So Q. Walker Lewis,

GT 19:27 Right.

Paul 19:28 Sorry. We haven't found evidence of his ordination. So, there's supposition that maybe he was, but no concrete evidence for Enoch. And none of the letters describe--he was definitely baptized and married to Mary Matilda Webster, who's a white member of the Lowell Massachusetts branch. But I haven't found concrete evidence for his ordination.

GT 19:55 Oh, okay. I think Connell believed that there was some pretty good evidence for that, but maybe not.

Paul 20:01 Connell suggests that it's a possibility. And you know, that may be true. We haven't found concrete evidence to substantiate that. Jordan Watkins at BYU is the one that's been doing the research. He did the bio at *Century of Black Mormons* for Q. Walker Lewis[11] and is also working on his son Enoch. Enoch's bio isn't loaded to the database yet, but Jordan has been working on it.

---

[11] See https://exhibits.lib.utah.edu/s/century-of-black-mormons/page/lewis-quack-walker

Moroni Able

GT 20:23 Okay. Okay. Who's this Moroni? That was somebody I hadn't heard about?

Paul 20:28 Sorry. So I thought you were referring to Elijah Able's son Moroni and he is ordained to the priesthood in 1871, in Ogden.

GT 20:37 Okay, way after the supposed ban, right?

Paul 20:40 Yes. And it's a deathbed ordination. But, nonetheless, there's no indication that his race is seen as a barrier. He falls ill, and I think it's his sister, Annie Able, who writes this, and it's published in the Ogden newspaper, that he falls ill. He's sick for several weeks. And he calls for the elders to give him a blessing. And at the same time that they bless him for health, they ordain him an elder in the priesthood.

GT 21:14 Oh, wow.

Paul 21:14 And that was not atypical in the 19th century, to give deathbed ordinations for young kids. The notion was you want them to have the priesthood as they pass into the next life. The Church stops that practice by the end of the 19th century. But it was pretty common in the 19th century. It's a last rite of sorts, that you want this person, a male person to have the priesthood as they go into the next life. And so, deathbed ordination was a thing. And Moroni Able,[12] Elijah Able's son receives a deathbed ordination and it's published in the newspaper, and no one seems to have an issue with it.

GT 22:06 In 1871. That's interesting.

---

[12] See https://exhibits.lib.utah.edu/s/century-of-black-mormons/page/able-moroni

Enoch & Elijah Able III

GT 22:09 Then Elijah's grandson, who was also Elijah, right?

Paul 22:13 Correct.

GT 22:13 [He] was ordained.

Paul 22:14 [He was ordained] in 1935 in Logan.

GT 22:18 Okay. Not a deathbed ordination.

Paul 22:21 Not a deathbed, no. And he lives the rest of his life as a practicing Latter-day Saint, as a priesthood holder. He's passed as white by that point.

GT 22:29 Okay,

Paul 22:30 His father, Enoch Able,[13] has passed away. And the early census record, the 1900 census record, defines Elijah--so it would be Elijah, III,[14] really, defines him as black in 1900, along with all the children in Enoch's family. Enoch dies in 1901. And he had married a white woman. And so, time and distance really account for a person's ability to pass as white. So, the black person in the family, the father, is now dead. The white mother is still alive. The kids grow to adulthood. The 1910 census, I believe, he's described as mulatto, and then in 1920, white. In every subsequent census after that, [he's] described as white. And the living memory of the black father is gone. Interracial marriages means that their skin was likely lighter than some African Americans and [he] moves away.

---

13 See https://exhibits.lib.utah.edu/s/century-of-black-mormons/page/able-enoch

14 See https://exhibits.lib.utah.edu/s/century-of-black-mormons/page/ables-elijah-r

GT 23:44 Did he live in Utah, at this time?

Paul 23:46 In 1935, when he's ordained, he's in Logan. He's baptized in Idaho, and then moves back to Logan, where he had grown up, and that's where he's ordained in 1935, and then moves to Montana. And that's where he passes away. I think it's in the 1960s. And his funeral is held at the LDS chapel in--I'm trying to remember the town, now. Anyway, his grave is there in Montana, and his whole funeral service is conducted by the bishop. I don't think anyone knows that they are burying the grandson of the faith's first black priesthood holder.

GT 24:32 Well, even Elijah was pretty light-skinned. Is that right?

Paul 24:35 Right.

GT 24:35 But didn't everybody know he was black?

Paul 24:37 Correct. He never passed as white. So, his death record in Salt Lake, his burial record in Salt Lake, includes the word 'colored' in the column where normally you're supposed to record the person's next of kin, they wrote the word 'colored.' And every census record describes him as he either Mullato or Quadroon. So, always defining him as racially, not white, and some percentage of black African ancestry. So, he never passes [as white] and he's understood in Church records, as well as public records, to be colored or black, or of black African ancestry, for his entire life. But his children, so his wife Mary Ann,[15] Elijah Able's wife, is also a mixed racial ancestry. Some of his children pass as white, some don't. But grandchildren, in particular, pass as white.

GT 25:48 Elijah Able, III, was he able to get a temple marriage, or sealing?

---

[15] See https://exhibits.lib.utah.edu/s/century-of-black-mormons/page/able-mary-ann-adams

Paul 25:54 I don't know that he ever applied. He was married twice, and neither of those are temple marriages.

GT 26:01 Okay. Yeah. But we don't know if he tried.

Paul 26:04 I don't know that he tried. I have no evidence of that. We couldn't find membership record for his second wife. I don't think she was LDS.

GT 26:13 Okay.

Paul 26:13 But she's living with him in Montana. And he's a practicing Latter-day Saint, as far as we can tell, because, like I said, his funeral, everything's published in the Montana newspaper. It's held in the LDS chapel. His fellow ward members are participating, singing songs, all of those kinds of things. So, just a normal Latter-day Saint funeral.

GT 26:40 Wow. This is why we like to talk to Paul Reeve. He's an encyclopedia. (Chuckling)

Paul 26:44 (Chuckling)

Warner McCary

GT 26:47 All right. Isaac Van Meter, Elijah Able, Walker Lewis, Enoch Lewis, Warner McCary. Can you talk about him?

Paul 26:57 Yeah. We I don't believe he was ordained to the priesthood.

GT 27:02 Really? You're killing me, Paul.

Paul 27:04 No, I don't think there's any evidence. In fact, I think there's pretty strong evidence that he wasn't, simply because of the interview that takes place with him and Brigham Young in March of 1847 at Winter Quarters. Basically, William [Warner] McCary says, "Look, I don't have any position of authority here." And he's basically saying [that] it's because I'm of a different color.

Paul 27:31 And that's when Brigham Young responds to him by saying, "Look, we don't even discriminate in distributing priesthood authority. We have one of the best elders, an African in Lowell, a barber," referring to Q. Walker Lewis, who we already talked about. So, in other words, if William McCary had the priesthood, there's no reason to point to Q. Walker Lewis. They would have said, "Well, yeah, you have the priesthood. See, we don't discriminate. You're ordained to the priesthood." Instead, he cites Q. Walker Lewis, as his example, that the Church doesn't discriminate in distributing priesthood authority. So, I think it's a pretty strong indication that he wasn't ordained. The only evidence is a belated remembrance back, in, I think it's the Voree Herald. So, separated by time and distance from the actual events, and it's a belated remembrance that suggested that Orson Hyde ordained him. And we've found no evidence that that's the case. And in fact, I think the interview with him and Brigham Young strongly suggests otherwise.

GT 28:46 That's what I had heard was that Orson Hyde had ordained him, but you think that's not true?

GT 28:49 That's not true. Like I said, the evidence for that is of a Voree Herald [article,] a Strangite publication and separated by several years from the events, and we're not even sure who the author of that suggestion is. So, people had, I think, given that report too much credibility, and we found no evidence of ordination.

GT 29:25 Oh, Paul. You're killing me. I was like, "Oh, there were six men ordained" and now you've just shot down, kind of Joseph Ball and Warner McCary. I'm trying to remember who the sixth one was.

{End of Part 1}

Russell Dewey Ritchie

Paul 00:56 So we have other people who have who pass as white in the database. In the database, we have a couple of cases where people, Latter-day Saints in the 21st century have written to us and said, "Hey, we have African ancestry in our DNA in the 21st century, and we think it traces back to ancestor X or Y, and if so, we would love to have them included in the database." And we've done the research and there have been other examples like that. Russell...

GT 01:34 Stephenson?

Paul 01:35 Russell Dewey Ritchie is in the database,[16] and he is ordained in 1971. He's in his 70s. And his father was formerly enslaved. So, he's the son...

GT 01:53 Did you say 1871 or 1971?

Paul 01:54 Correct, 1971, 1971. His father was born into slavery. So, this is the son of a slave. He was ordained in 1971. But, you know, he passed as white by that point. His father is likely the result of interracial rape and born into slavery,

GT 02:21 Because the slaveholders used to purposely impregnate slaves to get more slaves, right?

Paul 02:26 Correct.

GT 02:27 Is that probably what happened?

Paul 02:28 Well, I don't know the intent. The family has done all kinds of DNA work in this particular case. And so Russell's father,

---

[16] See https://exhibits.lib.utah.edu/s/century-of-black-mormons/page/ritchie-russell-dewey

Nelson Holder Ritchie[17] is the descendant of a white enslaver, and a black enslaved [mother.] And the circumstantial evidence suggests that it was more than likely an interracial rape and she becomes pregnant, is sold into Missouri. That's where Nelson Holder Ritchie is born. And then he shows up in the 1860s, in the home of a man by the last name of Ritchie in Kansas, who runs a stop on the Underground Railroad. And Nelson takes that as his last name. He fights in the Civil War on the side of freedom. He's a product of an interracial rape, more than likely. And then after the Civil War, he establishes a livery stable and hotel in Great Bend, Kansas, marries a white woman. Missionaries from the Church of Jesus Christ of Latter-day Saints take room and board at his hotel. You can predict the rest of the story. The family converts, they moved to Utah. Nelson and his wife, Annie Kellen Russell, apply to be sealed to each other. They apply for a temple admission in 1909 and are prevented because Nelson is black, and his bishop says "No. You can't." And they appeal and they say, "But our two oldest daughters have already been sealed in the Salt Lake Temple."

GT 04:20 Oh, wow.

Paul 04:21 And they had. They had. So they are, then, the product of two generations of interracial marriages, because Nelson's wife, Annie is white. He's a formerly enslaved man. Their children are light enough to pass [as white.] The two oldest daughters had moved out of the home, weren't living in the same ward, found people to marry and went to the Salt Lake Temple. No one had any questions about it. So, they were sealed. So, when Nelson and Annie wanted to be sealed as well, they said, "Well, our two oldest daughters are sealed." The bishop said "I don't care. I'm not letting you go," and never gave them a recommend. They had nine kids and every one of the kids either in life or by proxy after death received priesthood ordination and temple admission before 1978. One of the daughters is a Relief Society president in Layton, Utah

---

[17] See https://exhibits.lib.utah.edu/s/century-of-black-mormons/page/ritchie-nelson-holder

and sealed to her husband, and passes away in 1976. The daughter of a slave dies in Utah as a temple worker in 1976.

GT 05:32 Wow.

Paul 05:33 The whole family, in other words, it's just one experience after the next. The youngest son is Russell, and he's not ordained to the priesthood when he turns 12. He was 11 when his parents are denied temple admission. So, I only presume that the same bishop said, "I'm not ordaining your son to the priesthood." He eventually moves out, goes to California, becomes a pharmacist, marries his wife in the Presbyterian Church eventually returns to the Church of Jesus Christ of Latter-day Saints. I have no idea what story he tells his bishop as to why he's not ordained to the priesthood. But I found the ordination records, all in the same year, his Bishop first ordains him...

GT 06:20 Now wait a minute. Let me back up with here because you said that he married his wife in the Presbyterian Church. Did he join the Presbyterian Church?

Paul 06:28 I have no indication that he joined, but his wife was not LDS.

GT 06:32 Okay. And so, does it sound like he got rebaptized, or no?

Paul 06:36 No. He was already a member.

GT 06:39 Okay.

Paul 06:39 No, no reason given.

GT 06:41 I mean, I guess that it would be easy enough story to be like, "Well, I'm inactive. I'm a kind of a Jack Mormon and my wife's Presbyterian. Yeah, that's why I didn't get ordained." I mean, that would probably be a pretty easy story, a lot easier than, "Well, my grandpa's black, or my father."

Paul 06:55 And I don't even know what he understood about why he wasn't ordained. I have no indication. I don't know if they even understood that their father was formerly enslaved. I don't know what the parents said. I don't know how much they understood about their own father's racial identity. There's just no indication. The dad dies. Nelson dies in 1913. And so, his wife, Annie Cowan Russell waits a decade and then goes to the Salt Lake Temple, and has her husband sealed to her posthumously.

GT 07:35 And there's no race record on that card.

Paul 07:38 No!

GT 07:39 Because we don't look at race.

Paul 07:41 She's white. So, temple policy, in place at the time, was supposed to prevent that from happening. But the entire family demonstrate the impossibility of policing racial boundaries in life, let alone after death. And so, she just waits a decade and then has him ordained to the priesthood, goes to the temple, has him sealed to her posthumously. And all the rest of the family, all the kids marry white spouses. They raised their families as Latter-day Saints. The grandson of one of the daughters, or excuse me, Nelson Holder Ritchie's grandson is actually the quarterback at BYU in 1945.

GT 08:24 No way.

Paul 08:25 Yeah. So, the grandson of an enslaved man is a quarterback of the BYU football team.

GT 08:31 What was his name?

Paul 08:33 Rex Olsen.

GT 08:34 No way.

Paul 08:34 Yeah, yeah. And, he was ordained to the priesthood. No one is cognizant of this. And so those generations all had passed as white. They still have African ancestry in their DNA, because this family contacted me and said, "We would like our ancestor included in your database." And they had done extensive DNA research by the time they even contacted me. And so, for us, it was a matter of tracing the historical record, verifying the evidence. And it's a remarkable family story that demonstrates--in fact, I open the book with Nelson Holder Ritchie. He's in the introduction to the book...

GT 09:18 Wow!

Paul 09:18 ...to demonstrate the impossibility of policing racial boundaries. So, like I said, his youngest son, then in California, returns to the LDS faith and was ordained a deacon at age 71.

GT 09:37 Wow.

Paul 09:37 And then a couple of months later, [he was ordained] a teacher, a couple of months later a priest, and then a couple of months later an elder. Eventually, he moves to Roy, Utah becomes a High Priest. He moves to Arizona and is a temple worker, until he passes away in the 1980s. So, think how long slavery cast a shadow, the son of an enslaved man passes away as a temple worker in the 1980s in Arizona.

GT 10:09 That's really hard to believe.

Paul 10:10 Yeah, it's pretty remarkable.

GT 10:12 Wow. And that's how you start the book.

Paul 10:14 I started the book with that family, just to demonstrate the impossibilities of policing racial boundaries and [I] try to get the reader to think about, well, what is race? Is it something biological? Is something that's passed through the blood, like people said in the 19th century? Or is it just simply something we have made up in our minds, to try to distinguish between people who look like us and people who look different from us, and use it to justify discriminatory policies across the long course of human history?

Black Pete

Interview

GT 10:51 Wow. That brings up two questions. I want to finish up the first six that I thought I had identified, that you've already [been] shooting some holes in. Hopefully, you don't shoot a hole in this one. But Black Pete, that was the last one I couldn't remember. Would it be safe to say that Black Pete was the first black Mormon?[18]

Paul 11:11 Yes, yes. Yeah.

GT 11:13 So tell us that story. And do you think he was ordained?

Paul 11:16 So he is baptized in Kirtland. I mean, there's no early records. So, this is 1830. And you have the Latter-day Saint missionaries--I mean, most of your listeners probably know that story. The missionaries pass through the Kirtland region. And they convert a whole group of people. And I think amongst them is a formerly enslaved man that's only known in the written record as Black Pete.[19] But the researcher for *Century of Black Mormons*, Matthew McBride does the research on him and identifies him as a formerly enslaved man, enslaved to the Kerr family.

GT 11:59 I think Mark Staker figured that out.[20]

Paul 12:06 Well, you know...

GT 12:08 Or did he get that from McBride?

---

[18] See https://gospeltangents.com/2017/03/03/black-pete-former-slave-becomes-first-black-mormon/

[19] See https://exhibits.lib.utah.edu/s/century-of-black-mormons/page/peter

[20] See https://rationalfaiths.com/black-pete-early-mormonism/

Paul 12:10 Well. Matt's research is after Mark Staker's. So, Staker does include him as Black Pete in his book.

GT 12:24 Yeah.

Paul 12:24 And, his conversion and all those kinds of things are there. We don't think that he was ordained to the priesthood.

GT 12:34 Really?

Paul 12:34 Yeah. Yeah.

GT 12:35 Didn't he serve a mission in Ashtabula, Ohio? Because there's a newspaper article Mark told me [about.] I remember.

Paul 12:44 Hmmm.

GT 12:45 It said he had served a mission[21] and it was in the Ashtabula Journal. I don't remember what the name of the article was. He told me that on my podcast. I remember that.

Paul 12:53 Okay. Well, then we should follow that up. We should follow that up. If we miss something, then we can correct it.

GT 13:01 Well, I will say what Mark said, and I'll provide a link to that, as well. But what Mark said was [that] there were newspaper reports, I'm pretty sure it was in Ashtabula, that called him a leader among the people, a leader and a chief. I remember, because there was kind of a play on the Lamanite chief, Indian Chief. I thought he had served a mission between December of 1830 and February of 1831. And Mark says, there's no smoking gun. There's no certificate. I don't even know if they would have had those in 1830. But Mark says it seems likely that he was ordained. Mark's case was [that] a lot of times in 1830, especially men were ordained or

---

[21] See https://gospeltangents.com/2017/03/05/black-petes-mormon-mission-in-1831/

baptized and ordained simultaneously. And being such a small church, it would make sense that Black Pete might have been [ordained], because he was seen kind of as a leader. Mark also says he believes that Black Pete brought speaking in tongues[22] into the Church, which I think is really exciting. But, yeah, I thought there was some information there, because Mark says, we don't have a smoking gun. But it seems likely that Black Pete was ordained.

Paul 14:22 Yeah, that could be. I can't remember. I mean, it's been a while since I looked at how Matt McBride characterizes it for our biography in *Century of Black Mormons*.[23] So, I could leave that window open.

GT 14:37 Because you keep shooting all my windows Paul.

Paul 14:39 I know. I know. I know. And you're correct in terms of those earlier [times.] There are no certificates. There's no formal bureaucracy to even track this and so the earlier you go, even baptismal records are non-existent. And so, you're reliant upon a missionary happening to keep a diary and then record the names of those who they baptized. So, it's sporadic at best in terms of those early records.

GT 15:14 I mean, we can't even officially say who the first six were. I know Michael Marquardt has tried to do that.[24] We did a podcast about that. But yeah, we're not even 100% sure who the six people were who baptized on April 6, 1830.

Paul 15:26 Correct. Yeah. So yeah. So, the record keeping was not great and remains spotty, especially baptisms of enslaved people in the South. We've identified 26 people who were enslaved

---

[22] See https://gospeltangents.com/2017/03/03/black-pete-former-slave-becomes-first-black-mormon/
[23] See https://exhibits.lib.utah.edu/s/century-of-black-mormons/page/peter
[24] See https://gospeltangents.com/2019/04/who-were-original-6-in-1830/

at the moment of baptism, but I think the number is probably higher than that. It's just that the records don't survive to substantiate that.

GT 15:52 Okay.

Paul 15:53 At least 26 enslaved people were enslaved at the moment of baptism.

GT 15:59 Wow. That's interesting.

One Drop Rule

GT 16:01 Now, I want to go to one more point, and then we'll jump into your book. You had just mentioned that it was impossible to police a person's DNA, the one drop rule. I had Joe Jessop[25] on recently. And he, in my podcast said, there were three pillars of fundamentalism: polygamy,[26] the race ban,[27] and Adam/God theory.[28] These are the three [pillars.] And you know, that might differ depending on your polygamous group, or whatever. But I know in a recent Sunstone presentation, I'm trying to decide whether I should say his name. There is somebody I am trying to get on my podcast. I'll leave him vague for now. But he was a member of the Apostolic United Brethren. And, as I understand it, he had done a DNA test and found out he had black ancestry, and was basically excommunicated from the AUB, because of that black ancestry, which I personally find appalling. But it goes to this one drop rule. Obviously, we didn't really have that technology until say, 2000, to even test if somebody had black ancestry. But apparently, you can get kicked out of fundamentalist groups by having one drop. Any comments on that?

Paul 17:34 Wow. Well, that's not my research expertise. But I think the point that I made earlier, the *Century of Black Mormons* database just demonstrates the impossibility of trying to police that. I mean, now we can do DNA.

GT 17:54 And they'll kick you out, apparently.

Paul 17:58 Apparently, but for what purpose?

---

25 See https://gospeltangents.com/people/joe-jessop/
26 See https://gospeltangents.com/lds_theology/polygamy/
27 See https://gospeltangents.com/mormon_history/racial-priesthood-temple-ban/
28 See https://gospeltangents.com/lds_theology/adam-god-theory/

GT 18:01 To keep it pure. Keep the white race pure, right? I mean, I know that's a racist thing to say. But I mean, that's what it is. Right? It's ugly. It's ugly.

Paul 18:09 That's apparently the justification. I mean, I don't know.

Hardest Book Paul Has Written

GT 18:16 So all right, well, let's talk about race and priesthood. You gave a presentation at Writ & Vision about a week ago, with Darius Gray. And one of the things that I found really interesting was you said this was it the hardest book you've ever written. I guess you haven't written a lot of books.

Paul 18:43 Yeah, I mean, just in terms of hardest book I've ever written simply because I am writing as a Latter-day Saint to fellow Latter-day Saints. So that was not my typical approach in my scholarship. I'm typically writing for an academic audience, not necessarily for a Latter-day Saint audience. And then, also, sort of just identifying myself as a Latter-day Saints, inserting me into the narrative is something I'm not accustomed to. So, because of that, it made it really challenging for me. Yeah, it was hard to figure out the voice for this narrative. And I struggled at first. I sent three draft chapters to the editor at Deseret Book, Lisa Roper, who was fantastic to work with. I didn't want to get too far into the manuscript and have Deseret Book say, "No, that's not where we're looking for."

Paul 20:26 And so I said, "Hey, Lisa, can you look at these three first chapters and just give me an indication of what you think?" And Lisa is a phenomenal editor. I just had a great experience working with her. And she was she's really diplomatic. So, what I'm describing is not what she said. But it was basically the message that she conveyed.

Paul 20:52 She basically said like, "You're keeping your reader at arm's distance. This is dry and sterile. And you're trying for academic objectivity. And it just reads like you're holding your reader out here at arm's length." And she was absolutely correct. I don't think much of those first three draft chapters made it into the final manuscript. I basically had to start over, in other words. And I had to figure out my voice and figure out how I'm going to approach this. And it was difficult. So that's what made it the most difficult book I've written, is just trying to figure out how I'm going to speak as a Latter-day Saint to a Latter-day Saint audience, which was just not something I'm accustomed to.

GT 21:16 Yeah. Well, the other thing that you said was that Deseret Book approached you and said, "We want you to write a book," and what was your reaction?

Paul 21:26 Well, I was really skeptical, and I said that, I think, the first time Lisa approached me, [which] was in 2018, at the Mormon History Association Conference in Boise, where she...

GT 21:41 You were president at that one, weren't you?

Paul 21:42 No, no, I was president at the next one. So, I was on the board. I was president at the Salt Lake conference.

GT 21:49 Was it Patrick Mason?[29] Was he president?

Paul 21:51 Yeah, Patrick Mason was president in Boise. And then I was president at the Salt Lake conference the following year. And I just expressed skepticism that Deseret Book would be willing to publish something that I wrote on race and the priesthood.

GT 22:09 Because they didn't publish your first book, Religion of a Different Color.[30] Did they stock it, even?

Paul 22:16 I think, initially, they did. I think they did carry it on their shelves. I mean, obviously, I'm in an academic position. So, for it to count towards tenure, promotion, anything like that, I have to publish with an Academic Press.

GT 22:31 So, Deseret Book won't help you professionally.

---

[29] See https://gospeltangents.com/people/patrick-mason/
[30] Can be purchased at https://amzn.to/34nKRRI

Paul 22:35 No, not at all. And I wasn't interested in publishing with them because it doesn't count professionally for me, and I have to get an academic press. And so, Oxford published *Religion of a Different Color*. But, Lisa approached me about this. And she described the "Let's Talk About" series that they were envisioning. And she laid out their big picture vision of a series that was kind of modeled on Oxford's Short Introduction series, where they write short introductions to a topic, so like...

GT 23:09 Patrick did something with peace and violence.

Paul 23:11 Yes, a short introduction to religion and violence, or Mormonism and Violence.[31] I can't remember. But yeah, that's an example. I think his was not an Oxford series.[32] But there are other presses that have these short introduction series. And so, they wanted that model, but aimed not an academic audience, but at a general Latter-day Saint audience, devoid of academic jargon, but still with all of the sources and footnotes and the academic credentials, but still speaking to a lay Latter-day Saint audience. They wanted to tackle topics that are sometimes seen as controversial, to give Latter-day Saints something a little bit more than the Gospel Topics Essays,[33] to sink their teeth into. So, when she described the series, I was intrigued. I think that's a good idea. I liked the vision that she articulated. But I, nonetheless, expressed my skepticism that something that I wrote [that] Deseret Book would be willing to publish on race, just because I didn't think they would be willing to go where I would want to go. And Lisa reassured me that they wanted to be open and honest and "Hey, please give us a chance," is, I think, what I remember. "Hey, we would really like to try this out." They started this series with other books and they re-approached me and said, "We're still interested." One of my

---

[31] See https://amzn.to/3M06DAS

[32] It was published with Cambridge University Press.

[33] See https://www.churchofjesuschrist.org/study/manual/gospel-topics-essays/essays?lang=eng

conditions was, "You have to read Brigham Young's 15 February 1852 speech and know that I will be quoting from it. You can't come to me after the manuscript is completed and say, 'Hey, you can't say that.'" So I said, "You have to be aware of what I will be quoting." And they agreed to that.

GT 25:20 They read the speech.

Paul 25:22 Yeah, they did.

GT 25:22 Have you published that, yet?

Paul 25:23 They did.

GT 25:24 Because that's coming up in your next book, isn't it?

Paul 25:29 It is. Yeah. Yeah.

GT 25:30 I've been waiting for that speech for six years.

Paul 25:31 [It's] a separate project. But yeah, that will be coming out. We'll make all of those speeches publicly available.

GT 25:38 We will have you on again.

Paul 25:39 Yeah. (Chuckling) I will look forward to that. Anyway, I produced the manuscript, and I mean, it now exists.

Wilford Woodruff "One Drop" Problem

GT 25:53 And one thing I want to talk about with that speech-because I think it's amazing--because it deals, well, I don't want to say it deals with one drop, but there's a one drop problem, I guess we'll say. I believe and correct me if I'm wrong. Wilford Woodruff had quoted Brigham Young as saying something about one drop in the speech. But you said Brigham Young never actually said that.

Paul 26:23 Right.

GT 26:23 So tell us about that little issue.

Paul 26:25 Sure. So, Wilford Woodruff is a legislator in the 1852 territorial legislature. He attempts to capture Brigham Young's 5 February speech in longhand. He captures roughly 800 words of a 3000-word speech. And I think he gets the general sense of the speech pretty good but makes (I think) some critical mistakes. And one of those critical mistakes is he introduces the language of one drop into his version of the speech. And we then found the Pitman shorthand version, which LaJean Carruth, who's employed by the Church of Jesus Christ of Latter-day Saints Church History Department, transcribed it, based on the Pitman shorthand version, which was recorded by George Watt. And so that's how we know [that] we have a much longer speech than what Woodruff captured. And [we know] that Woodruff introduced some critical errors into his version.

GT 27:32 The problem is, people have been using Woodruff's version for a century.

Paul 27:36 That's right.

GT 27:36 We still we still don't have this speech yet.

Paul 27:39 Yeah. {chuckles} We're working on it. We're working on it. It will be publicly available. Yeah, so that's right. Most scholars had relied upon it and Woodruff doesn't date it, either. So that led to confusion as to the chronology of events at the legislative session. He doesn't date it as 5th of February. He just sticks it in his journal with no date. And so that also led to confusion amongst scholars. So, we now know it's a 5th of February speech, and we have the full Pitman transcription. And we will have them side by side, the Woodruff version versus the Pitman transcription version.

GT 28:22 Okay.

Paul 28:22 So scholars can compare across columns.

GT 28:26 Nice.

Paul 28:26 Yeah. And the Pitman version has, "No one of African ancestry can hold one jot or tittle of priesthood." And I think that's...

GT 28:40 Jot sounds a lot like drop.

Paul 28:41 I think Woodruff is going with one drop, right? And the speech says one jot or tittle.

GT 28:51 Really, semantically, it isn't really that much better.

Paul 28:55 Well, but it's not one drop of African blood. It's "can hold one jot or tittle of priesthood." And so, he's not talking about African ancestry. He's saying, "If you have African ancestry, you can't hold one jot or tittle of priesthood." That is what the Pitman Version says. Woodruff gets "one drop of African blood." I think he gets confused there.

GT 29:20 Okay. Because one drop was a common phrase of the day...

Paul 29:24 It was.

GT 29:25 ...in dealing with slavery and that sort of thing, right?

Paul 29:27 It was. Right.

GT 29:30 This is where my US history is really rusty. Wasn't it Virginia, or someplace like that talked about one drop of African blood or something?

Paul 29:39 Well, so in the 1850s, enslavers were using the one drop rule for passing on slavery to the next generation.

GT 29:51 So, even if they raped the slave, then the [offspring] could still be a slave.

Paul 29:56 Based on the condition of the mother, right? So a white man raping a black woman, the condition of slavery passes through the mother. So, some states passed these one-drop rules in terms of slavery. They could have 99 white ancestors and one black ancestor, and they could still be enslaved. Then after Plessy versus Ferguson,[34] you have segregation running rampant across the United States. You have some states then trying to define, "How much African ancestry can you have for us to legally segregate you?" And so, in this case...

Paul 31:12 So then it became a segregation issue.

---

[34] Plessy v. Ferguson, 163 U.S. 537 (1896), was a landmark U.S. Supreme Court decision in which the Court ruled that racial segregation laws did not violate the U.S. Constitution as long as the facilities for each race were equal in quality, a doctrine that came to be known as "separate but equal."

Paul 31:14 It became a segregation issue. And so, some states, this is after slavery has died, so we're not talking about inheriting slavery. We're talking about who can legally be defined as black in some states, like the state of Virginia. So, you are remembering that correctly. The State of Virginia, during segregation, does pass a one drop rule, which legally defines someone as black, if they have one drop of African ancestry, in the State of Virginia. They are legally defined as black. It became a segregation issue.

GT 31:13 Wasn't Virginia, also, the Loving versus Virginia case?[35]

Paul 31:17 Correct.

GT 31:18 Virginia is all over this.

Paul 31:20 Yes. Yeah. There's a one drop chapter in the book.

GT 31:26 Oh, okay.

Paul 31:27 So, I addressed that in the book, because Latter-day Saints, then, are attempting [something similar.] It plays out in terms of temple admission and priesthood ordination. How much African ancestry can a person have? And I demonstrate a couple of examples where they're trying to figure this out. Across the course of the 19th century, they increasingly go with a one drop attitude. George Q. Cannon argues for basically a one drop policy in 1900. It's formally put in place in 1907. So, the Church does adopt its own one drop policy in 1907, simply stipulating that it doesn't matter how remote a degree African ancestry. So, a person could look white, but if they have African ancestry, then they are barred from the priesthood and temple admission, no matter how otherwise worthy

---

[35] Loving v. Virginia, 388 U.S. 1 (1967), was a landmark civil rights decision of the U.S. Supreme Court in which the Court ruled that laws banning interracial marriage violate the Equal Protection and Due Process Clauses of the Fourteenth Amendment to the U.S. Constitution. The case effectively legalized interracial marriage throughout the United States.

they may be, the policy says. So, it's not based on worthiness. It's based on race. And that's what they attempt to enforce from 1907 onward.

GT 32:40 I mean, I don't know if this is too inflammatory, but I'm going to say it. It reminds me of the yellow star that the Jews had to wear in Nazi Germany. Right? I mean, isn't that a similar idea?

Paul 32:56 Well, I mean, this is just an effort at trying to ferret out a racial identity. And, I opened with the Ritchie family, which demonstrates the impossibility of doing that.

GT 33:15 Because Hitler was trying to do the same thing with Judaism. Right?

Paul 33:19 Right. Right.

GT 33:20 It's just terrible.

Paul 33:21 Yeah.

{End of Part 2}

How Deep Into the Ban?

GT 00:40 Well, I can't wait for your book to come out. Show people how thick this book is. It's a tiny book, especially compared to your [other book.] How many pages is that?

Paul 00:53 Well, with all the notes and everything and the index, it's 161 pages. But, in terms of just the writing, the last page in the last chapter is page 133.

GT 01:08 Okay.

Paul 01:08 So it's short. And the chapters are short, too. This was also something that I struggled to adjust to. They wanted sort of short, pithy chapters, keep the reader moving. But I actually grew to enjoy it right after I got into it. And so, some chapters are three pages, four pages long. They address the issue, and then we move on.

GT 01:34 You could probably read that in about an hour I'll bet, or two hours, maybe.

Paul 01:39 A couple of hours. I mean, people have sat down and just read it. I mean, I'm getting texts from people. "Hey, I just bought this and read it in a couple of hours." So, Deseret Book does have the audio version available. And I think it's says it's like a four-hour thing, if you listen to it on full speed. You can ramp it up to double speed and be done in a couple of hours.

GT 02:05 Are you the narrator, or did they get somebody else?

Paul 02:07 I'm not, no, they got someone else.

GT 02:11 So, how much history can you put into just a 130 page book? Because I have a feeling your *Religion of a Different Color* is much more in depth, much more detailed than this. Is that true?

Paul 02:28 It absolutely is. Yeah, of course. So, you get much more in depth. I go into outside public perception of who Latter-day Saints were, in *Religion of a Different Color*. And this is, there is one short chapter on that in this book, but it's largely the inside story. *Religion of a Different Color* tries to demonstrate the way that outsiders perceived Latter-day Saints, racially, in the 19th century, as not white enough. And you don't get the full extent of that in this. This is largely the inside story of moving away from their own black Latter-day Saint converts, towards whiteness, and the way that the racial restrictions take on a life of their own across the course of the 19th century. So yeah, I have to be really selective in the examples that I choose. And Deseret Book basically said [I need to shorten the book.] Yeah, I mean, the manuscript that I turned in, they said, "You've got to cut 10,000 words," to fit their format.

GT 03:36 How many words is that, do you know?

Paul 03:38 I can't remember what it finally came in at, but I had to cut 10,000, from what I originally submitted. And, I said, "You're already asking me to submit something that's so short. And then you're asking me to cut 10,000?"

Paul 03:53 Really, what they said was, "Cut out the multiple examples in each chapter. So, pick an example that illustrates the bigger point." I struggled with that, at first, but I actually like how it turned out, because it gives you an example to sink your teeth into. It illustrates the bigger point of the chapter. Some chapters do include more than one black Latter-day Saint story. But that's the other thing that I tried to do in this book is draw upon *Century of Black Mormons*. So, the racial story, even in *Religion of a Different Color*, is largely told from the perspective of the white leaders who are making these racial decisions. Most of the way that the story has been told has just been, when did the racial restrictions come into place? How do they develop over time? And that's true in *Religion of a Different Color*. But what I try to do here is to demonstrate how those policies actually impacted black Latter-day Saints in the pews.

GT 04:59 Which is a story not told nearly enough.

Paul 05:01 Exactly. And *Century of Black Mormons* made that possible. So, I could draw upon biographies from the database and demonstrate, here's how this policy that's being implemented actually impacted black Latter-day Saints. And so, I try to include those experiences, so that you actually get a sense of these policies had real world consequences.

Rapid Fire Questions About Book

GT 05:35 I feel like I'm smarter than the average bear when it comes to this issue, especially. It's one of my favorite issues. It may not be my listeners issue, but I love this issue. So, let me just ask you about some people that I'm familiar with, and see if those stories are in the book. It's already sold out. I haven't been able to get a copy. It's selling like hotcakes, apparently. So, do you talk about Black Pete?

Paul 06:05 I mentioned him as the first black Latter-day Saint. Yeah.

GT 06:08 Elijah Able?

Paul 06:09 Yes.

GT 06:10 Warner McCary?

Paul 06:12 Yes.

GT 06:12 Oh, you do? Yeah. Because he's the problem. Between him and the Enoch Lewis' mixed race child, I believe that was really what caused Brigham Young to reconsider.

Paul 06:25 I think you're right. I think you're right. And so, I deal with both of those experiences here as pivotal in turning Brigham Young's perspective. So, he's dealing with two cases of interracial marriages. And on December 3, 1847, so the end of 1847, after he's come to the Salt Lake Valley, and then going back to Winter Quarters, he's speaking out stridently against race mixing. And it seems to account for his change of direction on race and racial priesthood ordination.

GT 07:06 Because prior to that, we've got "a fine elder," Q. Walker Lewis in Lowell, Massachusetts.

Paul 07:11 Exactly.

GT 07:12 He was very favorable. And then those two, wasn't there a third one? I swear there was a third issue. Oh, I think it was Joseph Ball. Didn't he kind of get involved in polygamy with William Smith?

Paul 07:27 Yes, he did.

GT 07:27 But if he passed for white, I guess that wouldn't have been a race issue per se.

Paul 07:30 It doesn't seem to be a factor in what's going on in 1847. Yeah.

GT 07:36 You probably don't get into Joseph Ball.

Paul 07:38 No, no.

Orson Pratt Rejects Curse of Cain

GT 07:40 You did talk about the 1852 Legislature, apparently, because that was the big issue in writing the book. Right?

Paul 07:47 Correct.

GT 07:47 So how much detail can you get into that in just such a small book?

Paul 07:52 Not a lot of detail. But I do quote Brigham Young. I do quote Orson Pratt. They're in a debate over the laws that will govern white enslavers, who have brought their black enslaved people to Utah territory. And that produces some of Brigham Young's most strident sentiments about racial priesthood ordination, but also slavery in the 19th century. Orson Pratt is advocating for black male voting rights. And that helps us to account for some of the things that Brigham Young says in that 5th of February speech, because he says "We just as well give mules the right to vote here as negros and Indians." And he's pushing back against Orson Pratt who is advocating for black men being able to vote.

GT 08:44 And I will just remind people of our previous interview. I have one titled <u>Becoming a Fanboy of Orson Pratt</u>.[36] I still think it's cool that Orson Pratt was advocating for black voting rights in 1852!

Paul 08:58 It is cool, and he sticks to his convictions. And we have another new speech that will be in the next book, but, also, I just briefly quoted in this book. Orson Pratt in 1856 gives another strident anti-slavery speech wherein he says [that] we have no proof that Africans are descendants of "Old Cane."

---

[36] See <u>https://gospeltangents.com/2017/02/24/becoming-a-fanboy-of-orson-pratt/</u>

GT 08:58 Oh, really?

Paul 08:59 And that's the only justification Brigham Young ever gives for the racial restriction is Curse of Cain. Orson Pratt doesn't buy it. He says there is no proof. Hopefully we all know in 2023, Orson Pratt is correct. Black people are not descendants of Cain, but that was a long-standing justification for where black skin came from, calling black people as cursed and Brigham Young is bringing that into the faith with him and giving it theological weight, in this case.

GT 09:55 See that flies in the face of biblical literalism. Right?

Paul 09:58 That's right.

GT 10:00 I know quite a few biblical literalists in my ward.

Paul 10:04 Yeah.

GT 10:04 So, I think there are a lot of people that still would believe that Africans come from Cain.

Paul 10:08 Right. Yeah. If you read the book of Genesis, I mean, it doesn't actually say that. It was a biblical exegesis or a biblical way of interpreting. Some early scribes suggested that the mark that God put on Cain was black skin, but the Bible doesn't say that. [Early scribes say] the curse is somehow racial. The Bible doesn't say that. It was just standard interpretations, and then you throw in the Curse of Ham or Canaan, and that was justification for enslavement. And they said, "Well, the Bible supports slavery."

GT 10:52 The Israelites were slaves for a long time.

Paul 10:55 Right. So, they're using those standard justifications, in Brigham Young's case, to then suggest that there is a racial priesthood curse.

Death of Elijah Able

GT 11:10 Wow. I'm trying to remember. The next big issue to me, is there anything between 1852 and--well, you probably have the death of Elijah Able. That was probably a big deal, right? Do you talk about that in there?

Paul 11:27 Yeah, I do. Yeah. So just tracing how the racial restrictions develop over time and Elijah Able's application in 1879, to be sealed to his wife and to receive his endowment. So, just the indication that, as late as 1879, that racial restrictions are not firmly or unambiguously in place, because John Taylor doesn't know what to do with a black priesthood holder who received his Washing and Anointing rituals in Kirtland. He wasn't in Nauvoo when the endowment was introduced. He now is in Utah. His wife has passed away. He wants to be sealed to her and have his endowment and receive the rest of his temple rituals.

GT 12:08 You told me earlier. Who was it in 1871 that received the priesthood?

Paul 12:12 His son, Moroni.

GT 12:14 Moroni, but Moroni was on his deathbed.

Paul 12:15 Correct. But for Elijah Able...

GT 12:19 You gave it to my son.

Paul 12:20 Who knows what he even understands about the racial restrictions?

GT 12:23 Right.

Paul 12:24 Because his son has received ordination. He's ordained. He maintains this whole time that Joseph Smith sanctioned his priesthood. And so, his application in 1879, produces an investigation. And Joseph F. Smith is sent to interview him and comes back and reports that he's got his certificate dates. He knows who gave him his Washing and Anointing rituals in Kirtland. He's got all the information. He claims that Joseph Smith promised him that his priesthood would give him the blessings of the gospel. And he reports all of this, and John Taylor allows his priesthood to stand but doesn't allow him temple admission and basically says, "Well, maybe it's like some of the things done in the early days of the church."

GT 13:18 And we didn't know what was going on.

Paul 13:20 We didn't know what was going on. And then we sort of developed more refined understanding. And so, in his estimation, Brigham Young was correct. And Joseph Smith was the one that made the mistake in ordaining black men to the priesthood. And Brigham Young is correct in terms of restricting them from the priesthood.

GT 13:36 That's what John Taylor said.

Paul 13:37 Well, that's really what he's saying. Right? I mean, he's saying [that] in the early days of the Church, maybe we did things wrong, and then we had greater understanding. So, the greater understanding is Brigham Young.

GT 13:49 The restriction.

Paul 13:50 Instead of suggesting that Brigham Young got it wrong, and Joseph Smith got it right.

GT 13:54 Well, John Taylor said some pretty terrible things about blacks, right?

Paul 13:57 He did.

GT 13:58 How much do you cover that in there?

Paul 13:59 Yeah, it's not in here. It's in *Religion of a Different Color*. But John Taylor says they're their descendants of Satan. And so, he has his own understanding, as well. But he prevents Elijah Able from receiving his temple admission. But in 1883, Elijah Able goes on a third mission for the church and Joseph F. Smith, sets him apart, sends him to Ohio. He's 75 years old. He returns the following year and dies within two weeks as a faithful black priesthood holder.

Jane James' Attempt at Temple Blessings

GT 14:39 You probably talk about Jane James' attempt to get her temple blessings.

Paul 14:43 I do. Yeah.

GT 14:45 Can you share that really briefly?

Paul 14:46 Yeah, I mean, she's just appealing for her temple admission.

GT 14:52 That was due to Elijah's death, right?

Paul 14:54 Yeah, in 1884 she picks up where Elijah Able leaves off, basically. And she doesn't really until she passes away in 1908. She is repeatedly told no. She has given limited use recommends for the Salt Lake Temple, for the Logan Temple to perform baptisms for the dead. She had also participated in baptisms for the dead in the endowment house in 1875, along with several other black Latter-day Saints, but denied the crowning temple rituals of her faith.

GT 15:23 So, she could get in the basement of the temple, but that was it, basically.

Paul 15:26 That's it. Yeah.

GT 15:27 That's terrible to say.

Paul 15:28 Well, and Jane and her brother, Isaac, he joins her in Salt Lake and is rebaptized into the Church of Jesus Christ of Latter-day Saints in 1893. And they then are seen as prominent pioneer couples, and they're given cushion seats in the tabernacle, so prominent seats in the tabernacle, but barred from the temple.

GT 15:51 Wow. It's crazy.

Joseph F Smith Solidifies Restrictions

GT 15:53 I'm trying to think, is there anything else big? I guess Jane Manning's death in 1908. To me the next big step in the priesthood battle is President McKay. Is there anything in between Jane and President McKay?

Paul 16:08 Yeah, I mean, I make the case that Joseph F. Smith is really the one responsible for solidifying the restrictions in place. Because in 1908, he basically argues that Elijah Able's priesthood was declared null and void by Joseph Smith, himself.

GT 16:26 Which wasn't true.

Paul 16:27 No, it's not true, no. But he makes that claim. And so that becomes the new memory in the 20th century. The restrictions were always in place. God put them in place. They were there from the beginning. Man can't do anything about it.

GT 16:41 It all goes back to Joseph.

Paul 16:42 It goes back to Joseph. It even traces through the foggy mists of time into the eternities, right? And that becomes a memory for the 20th century. And the leadership believes that, and it becomes entrenched. And so that helps us to account for why it takes so long to unravel.

How 1978 Revelation Affected Black Women

GT 17:01 Okay. So the next big thing is probably when President McKay becomes Church president, and there's an issue in South Africa. Is that in the book?

Paul 17:13 I don't deal with his trip to South Africa. But I do talk about the lack of consensus in the McKay period, where you have people like Hugh B. Brown advocating for change, and people like Harold B. Lee entrenching around the restrictions. So, this is more of the 1960s? Yeah. So, once again, it's broad brushstrokes.

GT 17:40 Because you can't get fine detail in 130 pages.

Paul 17:43 You can't. So, I try to give life to the story, but also not the fine detail. And Matt Harris, I think, will fill us in on all of the detail in his book that's coming out. It really articulates the McKay administration as a lack of consensus with some people advocating for change and other people retrenching behind the racial restrictions. I talk about Bruce R. McConkie and *Mormon Doctrine,* Mark E. Petersen's talk in the wake of *Brown versus Board of Education*, at BYU. [I talked about] some in the leadership entrenching around segregation. And so, it helps us to understand how it gets perpetuated forward. And then, Spencer W. Kimball seems intent on building consensus and laying the groundwork for the 1978 revelation. And, once again, it's another brief chapter, and I actually...

GT 18:56 Do you talk about the Brazil temple?

Paul 18:57 I do. Yeah.

GT 18:58 Do you agree with Matt, that that was the first thing that President Kimball did to get rid of the ban?[37]

Paul 19:05 I mean, I think Matt's the expert on that. I think it's a significant factor in unraveling, absolutely. Yeah. And I'll leave it to Matt, to give us the full details on that. Once again, it's short here, but actually I quote Marion G. Romney, who says, "Look, the temple in Brazil was a significant factor here. Trying to figure out racial identity in a mixed racial country is next to impossible. And we're building a temple there." And he articulates that and so I quote him briefly.

GT 19:46 He's not one we usually associate with racial progress.

Paul 19:51 Yeah, no, and it's not--really I mean, he's just basically saying it's a significant factor in why the revelation came about. And so, I'm just quoting that. But the 1978 Revelation chapter is really framed by a black woman, Freda Lucretia McGee Bealieu. I wanted readers to understand that it's not just priesthood, but black women were barred from temple admission. And she was baptized in 1909, in a creek, outside of Tylertown, Mississippi. And in July of 1978, she's traveled 1000 miles to the Washington, DC Temple, to be sealed to her husband, who has predeceased her. And she's waited 69 years to get into a Latter-day Saint temple. And so, I wanted readers to appreciate how this impacted real life people. And I think she's a profound example, someone who had remained faithful for 69 years before she was allowed into LDS temple.

GT 20:59 Wow. That's too long. I wish it had never happened. I still wish.

---

[37] See https://gospeltangents.com/2019/12/brazil-influenced-od2/

Addressing Lingering Justifications of Ban

GT 21:05 You know, I look at places like the Community of Christ. I mean, it's not that they've got a stellar racial record, either. But they never had a ban, at least. The Strangites never had a ban. The Bickertonites, I think they had an apostle in the early 1900's that was black. And so, it didn't have to be this way. I hate it when I hear people say that well it was up to God and 1978 was just a magical year. I mean, how do you respond to people when they say those kinds of things?

Paul 21:36 So, the last part of the book, I mean, Deseret Book asked me to address some of the lingering justifications. And so, I do deal with that, and just try to unravel some of those justifications. I start out the book by simply quoting--Joseph Smith claims five revelations that stipulate that this gospel is to be preached unto every creature. That leaves no one out. The divine timeline is every creature and he's receiving those revelations as early as 1831. And they keep getting repeated. This gospel is to be preached unto every creature. That leaves no one out. There's no, "This is just God's timing." God's timing was [that] this is the last dispensation, and everyone is included. The revelations that Joseph Smith claims indicate that. Joseph Smith says that Jesus says to him twice, in 1831, "All flesh is mine, and I am no respecter of persons." So, you have to take those revelations seriously. The case that I make in the book is 1978 returns the Church to its universal roots.

GT 23:04 It's a restoration.

Paul 23:05 It's a restoration. Yeah, it is back to the original universalism. So, the structure of the book is just structured in three phases: open priesthood and temple, segregated priesthood and temples, and then a return in 1978 to the original universalism. And that's the exact structure. And so, if readers take nothing else away, I hope that they appreciate the evidence that the racial restrictions were not in place from the beginning. And the evidence is included, and the structure of the book is structured that way to illustrate that.

GT 23:43 Very cool. All right. Anything else you want to share on this? Buy multiple copies and give them to your friends.

Paul 23:55 Of course, I'd be happy about that. No, I don't think so. I mean, I hope readers appreciate it, and appreciate the fact that that Deseret Book was willing to publish it. And I think it's open and honest. It's an open and honest retelling. Obviously, it's short. So, it's not going to include everything.

GT 24:20 Your other book is for that. There were two books, right?

Paul 24:23 Right. And Matt's too.

GT 24:23 The one before and Matt's, too.

Paul 24:24 Yeah, and Matt's book. I mean, it's aimed at being accessible to the average Latter-day Saint.

GT 24:34 Let me ask you this. If a Church member said that the ban was racist, how would you react to that?

Paul 24:47 If the ban was....?

GT 24:48 If they said, "I think that the priesthood ban was racist."

Paul 24:56 Well, I'm not sure what you're saying.

GT 25:01 Well, there's an issue. I've talked with different people. Honestly, I believe that the ban was racist. I've had other people that say, "No, it wasn't racist. For whatever reason, God only knows. It's not racist. This is God's plan."

Paul 25:21 I see.

GT 25:21 How would you respond to both of those issues?

Paul 25:25 Yeah, yes. Well, I mean, I would ask them to engage with the evidence. And I hope this volume lays out the evidence. So, for example, I use Freda Lucretia Magee Beaulieu in that 1978 revelation chapter. She can answer the temple recommend questions exactly the same as a white person before June of 1978. The white person will be admitted to the temple and Freda denied. It's not based on worthiness, because she's answering the questions the same. It's based on race. That's racism. So, I'm not sure that people have fully come to terms with that. And I hope that by illustrating how these policies impacted the lives of real people, that it might prompt people to think more deeply about that. So, if you're making determinations based on a person's race, that's racism. If you're not making determinations based on their answer to temple recommend questions. So, you can answer the temple recommend questions, exactly the same, but you're barred because of your race, then that's racism.

GT 26:45 Okay. We're not judging people by the content of their character, but by the color of their skin.

Paul 26:51 Right. Or by their devotion to God. And President Russell M. Nelson has actually articulated that. He has said in recent speech, "Let me be clear. We are not judged based on our skin color. We are judged based on our devotion to God and His commandments." The racial restrictions worked exactly the opposite. President Nelson taught eternal truths. The racial restrictions violated those truths.

GT 27:22 Very good. And then the last question, I wanted to ask you, you had mentioned at that Writ & Vision meeting that they wanted you to use the word "I." "I believe." "I, I, I." I know that was hard for you. It seems like Deseret Book also were like, "These are the opinions of Paul Reeve. These are not official Church [positions]." Does that make it easy for, shall we say, more conservative members to write off the book and say, "Who cares what Paul Reeve thinks? I'm not racist. I think the ban came from God." How do you respond to that?

Paul 28:09 Yeah, well, everyone's going to have to make up their minds for themselves. But I hope it's based on evidence, and I think this book actually offers them the evidence. So, you're going to have to argue against the evidence. And yeah, so Deseret Book asked me to make it clear that I'm speaking for myself.

GT 28:28 Not for the Church. Not for Deseret Book.

Paul 28:30 And I would never pretend to speak for the Church. So, that's including "I" statements, right? These are things that I believe to be true. But I also believe that they're grounded in evidence.

GT 28:44 Okay, you wouldn't have a problem--I don't know if that's the right way to say it. But for people who just say, "Well, that's Paul's belief. I don't have to believe that." I mean, how would you respond?

Paul 28:56 Well, like I said.

GT 28:59 Grounded on evidence.

Paul 29:02 Certainly people don't have to believe anything that I say. That's up to them. But I hope they're willing to engage with the evidence. And this is documented. You know, new evidence has come to light even since *Religion of a Different Color.*

GT 29:18 I know! We've talked about it today. It's been amazing.

Paul 29:21 So, I'm hoping that they're willing to engage with that, and they make their determination based on the evidence.

GT 29:29 And so, final question, tell us about your upcoming book, and when do you think it'll be out? Do you have a name for it yet?

Paul 29:34 Yeah. It's called *This Abominable Slavery*. And it will just lay out the 1842 legislative session. Christopher Rich and LaJean Carruth are my co-authors for that. We tell the story of the Black Servant Code as well as the Native American Indenture bill that were passed by the 1852 Territorial Legislature. And [we] lay out that narrative story to lay out indigenous as well as African American slavery in Utah territory in the 19th century.

GT 30:13 And I will tell everybody, I've been waiting for at least six years.

Paul 30:17 It's been a long time. And we will also make all of those speeches that were newly transcribed, we'll make them publicly available.

GT 30:24 And will become even a bigger fanboy of Orson Pratt.

Paul 30:27 Yeah, I'm hoping that [comes out] within the next year.

GT 30:32 Okay. Yeah. Cool. Cool. Well, we will definitely love to have you back on here, Paul.

Paul 30:36 Sounds great.

GT 30:38 All right. Thanks, again, for being here on *Gospel Tangents*. I appreciate it.

Paul 30:40 Yeah, it's my pleasure. Thank you.

Additional Resources:

Check out our other interviews with Paul Reeve.

Dr. Paul Reeve on Black Mormon History in Utah

https://gospeltangents.com/2022/09/paul-reeve-discusses-race-ban/

009: Dr. Paul Reeve's Role in Race Essay
https://gospeltangents.com/2017/02/27/paul-reeve-wrote-the-race-essay/

008: Dating the LDS Temple and Priesthood Ban
https://gospeltangents.com/2017/02/26/dating-the-lds-priesthood-and-temple-ban/

007: Becoming a Fanboy of Orson Pratt
https://gospeltangents.com/2017/02/24/becoming-a-fanboy-of-orson-pratt/

006: The Black Mormon Scandals
https://gospeltangents.com/2017/02/22/the-black-mormon-scandals/

005: How did Joseph Smith Deal with Muslims? & Chinese & Indians?
https://gospeltangents.com/2017/02/19/how-did-joseph-smith-deal-with-muslims/

004: How did Others Deal with Slavery?
https://gospeltangents.com/2017/02/12/how-did-others-deal-with-slavery-blackhistorymonth/

003: <u>How Mormons Became a Racial Category</u>
https://gospeltangents.com/2017/02/09/how-mormons-became-a-racial-category/

Critiquing the LDS Gospel Topics Essays

Dr. Newell Bringhurst (left) & Dr. Matt Harris are co-editors of "The LDS Gospel Topics Series."

458: <u>Race, Priesthood, & Randy Bott</u>
https://gospeltangents.com/2020/11/race-priesthood-randy-bott/

457: <u>Racism in Mormon Scripture</u>
https://gospeltangents.com/2020/11/racism-mormon-scripture/

456: <u>Pros & Cons of Race Essay</u>
https://gospeltangents.com/2020/10/pros-cons-of-race-essay/

Darron Smith on Race, Religion, & Sport

Dr. Darron Smith, teaches Sociology & Public Health at University of
Memphis,

035: Overcoming "Nice" Racism
https://gospeltangents.com/2017/05/16/nice-racism/

034: BYU Protests
https://gospeltangents.com/2017/05/13/byu-protests/

033: How do Minorities fare at BYU?
https://gospeltangents.com/2017/05/10/how-do-minorities-fare-at-byu/

032: True & False Rape Allegations at BYU
https://gospeltangents.com/2017/05/07/true-false-rape-allegations-at-byu/

031: How BYU Could Improve the Honor Code for Black Students
https://gospeltangents.com/2017/05/04/how-byu-could-improve-the-honor-code-for-black-students/

030: Black Graduation Rates at BYU
https://gospeltangents.com/2017/05/02/comparing-byus-black-graduation-rates/

029: Disparities in Black/White Discipline
https://gospeltangents.com/2017/04/28/disparities-in-blackwhite-discipline/

028: The Student-Athlete Business
https://gospeltangents.com/2017/04/25/the-student-athlete-business/

027: Racial Portrayals of Christian Athletes
https://gospeltangents.com/2017/04/22/racial-portrayals-of-christian-athletes/

Russell Stevenson – Biographer of Elijah Abel, early black Mormon missionary

Russell Stevenson, Biographer of Elijah Ables

126: The LDS Church in Africa
https://gospeltangents.com/2018/02/12/lds-church-in-africa/

125: Elijah Ables' Attempt for Temple Blessings
https://wp.me/p8l6gx-ox

124: Why Brigham Changed his mind on Black Ordination
https://gospeltangents.com/2018/02/brigham-changed-mind-black-ordination/

123: Trouble in Cincinnati: Ables' Time in Ohio
https://gospeltangents.com/2018/02/04/trouble-cincinnati-ables-time-ohio/

122: Ables' Canadian Mission & Escape from the Mob
https://gospeltangents.com/2018/02/01/ables-canadian-mission-escape-mob/

121: Early Life of Elijah Ables
https://gospeltangents.com/2018/01/29/early-life-of-elijah-ables-blackhistorymonth/

Newell Bringhurst – Author of Saints, Slaves, and Blacks

Dr. Newell Bringhurst, author of several books on Mormon History

135: Critiquing the Gospel Topics Essays
https://gospeltangents.com/2018/03/13/critiquing-gospel-topics-essays/

134: Role of Women in 4 American Religions
https://gospeltangents.com/2018/03/10/role-of-women-in-4-american-religions/

133: More about Polygamy: Bennett, Bushman, & Compton
https://gospeltangents.com/2018/03/07/more-about-polygamy-bennett-bushman-compton/

132: Bringhurst's Approach to Controversy
https://gospeltangents.com/2018/03/04/bringhursts-approach-controversy/

131: Bringhurst on Bushman-Brodie
https://gospeltangents.com/2018/03/01/bringhurst-bushman-brodie/

130: Walker Lewis: Faithful Black Elder
https://gospeltangents.com/2018/02/26/walker-lewis-faithful-black-elder/

129: Warner McCary: Real Native Genius?
https://gospeltangents.com/2018/02/25/warner-mccary-real-native-genius/

128: How Lester Bush Debunked the Missouri Thesis
https://gospeltangents.com/2018/02/18/how-lester-bush-debunked-missouri-thesis/

127: Writing Saints, Slaves, and Blacks
https://gospeltangents.com/2018/02/dr-newell-bringhurst-saints-slaves-blacks/

Matt Harris – Black History WW2 to Present

Dr. Matt Harris, History Professor, CSU-Pueblo

161: Bruce R. McConkie Wrote Official Declaration 2!
https://gospeltangents.com/2018/06/01/bruce-r-mcconkie-wrote-official-declaration-2/

160: How Kimball Persuaded Apostles to Agree on Lifting Ban
https://gospeltangents.com/2018/05/29/how-kimball-persuaded-apostles-to-agree-on-lifting-the-ban/

159: Almost Famous! 1969 Black Ordination Nixed by Lee
https://gospeltangents.com/2018/05/26/almost-famous-1969-black-ordination-nixed-by-lee/

158: Hugh B. Brown's Attempt to End Ban in 1962!
https://gospeltangents.com/2018/05/23/hugh-brown-end-ban-1962/

157: Did Pres. McKay Try to Rescind Ban in 1955?
https://gospeltangents.com/2018/05/20/did-pres-mckay-try-to-rescind-ban-in-1955/

156: When, Where, & Why Did the One-Drop Rule Originate?
https://gospeltangents.com/2018/05/17/where-when-why-did-the-one-drop-rule-originate/

155: Before 1978: How LDS Leaders Handled Bi-racial Families in Brazil and South Africa
https://gospeltangents.com/2018/05/14/before-1978-lds-policies-for-bi-racial-families-in-brazil-south-africa/

Race Struggles at BYU 1965-1985

Dr. Matt Harris discusses the LDS race ban 1965-1985

353: Impact of Protests on Apostles
https://gospeltangents.com/2019/12/impact-of-protests-on-apostles/

352: BYU Law School Almost Lost Accreditation
https://gospeltangents.com/2019/12/byu-law-accreditation/

351: Civil Rights Investigation at BYU
https://gospeltangents.com/2019/12/civil-rights-investigation-at-byu/

350: Sports Protests Against BYU
https://gospeltangents.com/2019/12/sports-protests-byu/%20

349: Race & Religious Minorities at BYU
https://gospeltangents.com/2019/12/race-religious-minorites-at-byu/

348: How Brazil Influenced Official Declaration 2
https://gospeltangents.com/2019/12/brazil-influenced-od2/

347: Did Nixon & Carter Pressure BYU Over Race?
https://gospeltangents.com/2019/12/did-nixon-carter-pressure-byu/

Final Thoughts

You can get our transcripts at our amazon.com author page. I've got a link here, but just do a search for Gospel Tangents interview, and you should be able to find a bunch of them there. Please subscribe at Patreon.com/gospeltangents. For $5 a month, you can hear the entire interview uncut and for $10 you can get a pdf copy. We've also got a $15 tier where if you want a physical copy, I'll be the first to send it to you, so please subscribe at Patreon or on our website at Gospeltangents.com. For our latest updates, please like our page at facebook.com/Gospeltangents and also check our twitter updates Gospel tangents. Please subscribe on our apple podcast page tinyurl.com/GospelTangents, or you can subscribe on your android device. Just do a search for Gospel Tangents. Thanks again for listening. Click here to subscribe, here for transcript and over here we've got some more of our great videos. Thanks again.

9 7983 89 0 3 8 4 4 8